Australian ravens

By the same author:

Everything Falls In (2000)
Darkness Disguised (2002)
The Kurri Kurri Book of the Dead (2007)
After Han Shan (2012)

Australian ravens

Greg McLaren

PUNCHER & WATTMANN

First published in 2016
Published by Puncher and Wattmann
PO Box 441
Glebe NSW 2037

http://www.puncherandwattmann.com

puncherandwattmann@bigpond.com

National Library of Australia
Cataloguing-in-Publication entry:

McLaren, Greg

Australian ravens

ISBN   9781922186638

I. Title.

A821.3

Cover design by Matthew Holt

Printed by Lightning Source International

This project has been assisted by the Australian Government through the Australia Council, its arts funding and advisory body.

Australian Government

Australia | Council
for the Arts

Contents

Australian ravens

Blacksmiths

I took my great-grandfather's name

                          to usurp my own,

my father's —

              and here we are, barely into the '70s,

four generations of men

                   governing the salt water air

and the rot of the sandbar's seaweed

at Blacksmiths Beach:

                 Poppy, his son-

in-law, and his son-in-law, and his two boys,

                        trailing

behind them,

the sand complaining beneath our feet,

a cloth rubbed over a damp mirror.

                   The older men

are talking about The Works (steel, not Shakespeare),

their words circling life along the curved white beach;

the women have stayed inside, sitting over lemonades

under the tin roof

               of what's now a corner

of a beach-side carpark,

              trawling births

and concealing the past,

                 the family's stories already

falling into a wash of silence between the sea and the lake,

drifting loose from their speech,

a receding and beckoning shoreline.

Owl

At the back door landing
I'm three, in a tight blue parka,
staring into the aimless dark,

looking at where Dad and John are pointing,
seeing nothing but the uneven top of the side fence
where they swear there's an owl.
                                What's an owl?
I fix on Dad's finger,
and think there's an answer there –
I'll never get it
                now,

still looking for that owl, retracting my steps
through the hallway and shadowed family
to the dark blur outside, and what it is

I don't see there,
to find that bird in the flitting and fruitful night.

Abermain Quarry

Now it's filled entirely, level with the earth.
On Google Maps it's glazed with a spread
of dirt, and mushroomed with the canopies
of pixelated trees, and a waterhole

barely the size of a drowning.
Boxing Day afternoon, we filed down there,
away from family Christmas
along Tamworth Street, past the red brick

of the Mines Rescue Station,
to seek bottles and smash them,
for shits and giggles, against the sandstone
walling off the quarry from the school, or against

already broken bottles left by other kids,
a dumb archaeology, a sediment of boredom.
Other times we'd been there
collecting grazes and gouges,

dust and slivers in scabbed elbows and knees
as we scrabbled the hard slope.
The Abermain kids would get their bikes
down there somehow, in the days before

BMXs, and we'd be run off
the premises as ring-ins, outsiders, even though
all our fathers were born and learned
to hate there. The five of us, cousins and brothers:

Chris dead of a tumour just after thirty, John,
vanished eleven years, Graham we lost track of,
and Andrew, named for the pit-working
granddad none of us ever met,

silently buried and denied. We stand
at the edge and pick our way down, small specks
of coal beneath our skin, hardly noticeable,
even if you knew what to look for.

Siding

A disused rail siding,
the grass-covered platform
a sharp-edged mound of earth.

Loose clunks of coal, patches
of brown dirt, the gums' sparse shadow.
At the edge of the bush, crow calls

shush the wheeling song of magpies.
The odd car fizzes past, thirty-
somethings behind the wheel

born long after the mines closed down.
In the middle-distance, short
of those hills, it's eucalyptus haze,

not bushfire smoke, that distorts
the changing patterns of light between clouds
flickering on the low slopes. Even though

that light travels so quickly, scanning
for the outline of the road into the hills
is like looking into a hazy future.

I kick a spot of gravel, trying
to frame roughly where a photo was taken,
somewhere very near here, once.

Pit time

for Andy Bull

The mine whistles set the clocks
and buried the men.
A fire at Hebburn No.1,

and smoke palls
from the tunnel openings
like a drop-off

in union membership.
Kids and housewives clanged
pots and pans at scabs

on their way to the picket line.
Near the asphalt car park
by the railway,

and the low log fence,
the War Memorial's obelisk —
another stone, marking more men

beneath the ground.
In local museums in back rooms
of schools and libraries

hang turn-of-the-century photos:
aerial views of mine huts and pit heads,
taken atop the nearest hill.

Asbestos breathes in the rafters,
sepia drips from the corners.
My father's father

just shunted the coal skips,
went on strike when his mates did,
and stayed out of trouble.

At the age he was
when he was put on as a pit-boy,
I was thinking of cars, or trains,

and how far away and how quickly
that would take me
past that close ring of towns,

a picket-line of sacked workers,
rugged-up like my grandfather,
dying of organ failure

as the mines closed down
across the coalfields,
sitting on the verandah at Abermain,

gazing out at the bush
through the scaffolding of new houses
going up across the road. From the cutting

below street level, steam trains chew coal
from the mines to the port on the coast

and, thick as the black from a pit fire,
pour smoke from the ground.

Coon Island

Your finger over the Newcastle *Gregory's* —
the pale green there, in the entrance
to Lake Macquarie, of Coon Island,
its narrow tidal mudflats, its fat plank bridge

a swing creaking with utes, and the Awabakal
siphoned out of Swansea like a euphemism.
Soldier crabs hive back into the grey mangrove
grit at the slightest movement. A flap of colour

from the caravan park across the dirt road,
cars moving, tents going up, and in the annexe
of one of the vans, your grandmother's voice,

recalling her trip around Australia, when she saw
two aborigines fucking on a beach in daylight
in the middle of nowhere: *I know*

we treated them bad for two hundred years but when
we seen that, that's when I didn't have no more pity
for any of 'em.

Australian ravens

i.m. Noel Rowe

Five days, I was followed by ravens:
on fences along New Canterbury Road;
perched on a hospital's sandstone wall
at Paddington; in the air
above Villa Maria.

The flavour of salt is slight,
at the corners of my mouth:
there is a word I meant to say.
I could never get my mouth
to move wholly around it.

Here, the open church-front air,
in the company of friends,
a creaking wheel in the trees:
cockatoos swooping, heavy,
between buildings.

My hand makes a silent language
with my soft black hat:
skin against felt, turning
it slowly, a fidgetty symptom,
giving away nothing.

Early autumn light

for Shel and Ben
After Peter Kirkpatrick

If love is friendship written large,
then marriage is emotional skywriting,
Peter Kirkpatrick says,

and also, I suppose, a public mural, ongoing,
you add to with your families,
and pets, and a squillion kids,

and have your friends come over, say,
for a New Year's barbie,
and they daub in their little bit −

adding that deep, netty texture of living, eating,
drinking and talking with the people you choose
and don't choose, and would never

choose not to, sitting silently with them
in the shade on a sunny day
with the flies buzzing and the ipod hooked up

to the speakers, and somehow your glass empties
and fills, and your plate grows crumbs
and maybe party pies with plops of sauce,

and the little gold-brown skinks perch
on the fence like slim leaves, panting.
Remember how poetry brought you almost

together, but how a birthday succeeded: another
beginning, another marked-in-the-calendar
day of continuations, like the prospect

of a long and gorgeous life, or,
as seen through gums and pines lining the ocean
just east of here, of New York City:

may it be fruitful, big and fruitful, may you let
bagels be bagels.
So I wonder what else it is

I wish for you. And come up empty.
Other than what you have already,
other than yourselves, and sometimes

some of our company, for a very long time,
by which I don't necessarily
mean people who arrive for Friday dinner

and don't leave til four on Sunday arvo,
with winter approaching.
Still, even then, with the sun,

half-gold, lowering on the afternoon's horizon,
there's a sort of clarity, even as it's thinking
of nudging the hem of the west,

getting tucked in for the *first*
official night of funny business.
That honeyed glow there

in your eyes is also in the eyes of everyone
you've brought here to this open-air wedding,
marquee at the ready if things get tense

and weather threatens overhead.
We've come from all points of the compass:
driven, slept-over, stepped from boozy buses,

trailed across a route suggested
by whereis.com, and along the way,
the scent of someone

turning over the earth in their garden,
and then everything smells like renewal,
like a constant vow to continue,

which is, anyway, always only a beginning.
So, this day is a beginning,
a stretching-out like a view

from a hilltop of suburbs waking
in soft dawn light,
or like the ocean, calm and ambitious,

more vast than it knows.
All these likes remind me
of a stronger word: love.

If love can be a city, let it begin
to sprawl, in any season's light,
as warm as sun-browned sandstone.

And now the sun, drooping away in the west,
cooling the air, and the bridge that joins
this north side to the inner west,

on a day, well, like today, with you two wed,
reminding us of the impossibility
of ever knowing exactly how much

someone means to you, even the roughest dimensions,
trying to trace a limit, and finding none.

Honey

Walking home along New Canterbury Road
I pass under a eucalypt I can't name – the rumour
of honey, the frayed brake lining of magpies –

and I think of our walk
around Manly Dam the first week of summer,
the day heating and finally loosing its energy
in a brief drizzle,

cooling the water dragons curious as we are,
as they retreat only the distance
we approach, and the shower

so short that after your father calls
your mobile, worried about Christmas plans,
and then puts on your mum,
it's passed –

then there's something we've already left behind,
we stop and turn back a few paces, sensing
we've missed – what? a hum
like a distant generator,

                              or a narcissist's sigh –

and two yards above us, a swelling
in an ironbark, inhaling and exhaling bees:

and knowing next to nothing about bees,
unsure if they're natives
or feral imports, we watch —
                              some of them
burnished as museum medallions,
classic sheened bands of black and gold
pure as a home brand,

and others, their hive-sisters,
muffled stripes of dusky and tarnishing bronze
mixed with the colour of shit,

and, behind the honeycomb in the air
with summer dirt's tang as it lifts, glowing
with the sun's penumbra as it dips
behind the hill and trees —
                              the after-image
that lasts, as we look away again,
another thing gone from sight.

Waiting

for Shel, Ben and Will

The terminal oscillates on the dipping harbour,
the benches are bleached wood and late summer
afternoon skims over them;

and a scum of light flakes and catches on the waves.
A mural in pale, pacific blue: *We're improving wharf safety* –
girders and scaffolding behind it
bleed filthy rust. Off Kirribilli, the last

of the sun is a bright gold slick in the ferry's wake,
then a wash of shade past Bradley's Head.
The north's water frontages are the first

flecks of Sydney to slip into the dark.
A Canadian tourist bangs away at his silent neighbour
on the virtues of Kindle, fingering
his unresponsive keyboard. Clifftop trees lean

away from the water, the foliage tinted grey
from worry and salt. Manly's sudden skyline
over Middle Head is the advent
of a new civilisation, where Bruce Beaver's lines

trail in the breeze: magpies, pines, children
he never envied, the ocean's rusting spray.
Here, boy-men with bumfluff circuit the deck,

scanning the boat's horizon for talent.
I'm here to meet my expectant friend
at the terminal gates, and eddying through
the afternoon's crowd as it spills and mutters,

we're destined for pesto and gorgonzola.
After dinner, from the beach
to a bench by the cove,

we slurp at gelato, and gossip, giggling
over the autopsied past: talking shit,
you never know exactly how much
someone means to you.

On the way back, there's a rough swell
between the heads, and the gulls
appear from the black there, drawn out

by the ferry's tossing lights, and circle the boat,
giddy with hunger's reiteration; or else they vanish again

beyond the reach of the bulbs, steady
as a fade-out.
                    Back at the quay,
aching with happiness, and a little heartsore
for another, more distant friend, and waiting

for a bus home, there's the spew stink
of Friday night bus queues. Standing there,

that pungency becomes almost sweet,
thinking myself blessed with you: loyal,
constant and warm, and I'm spilling, for a while,
with hope.

Not being in Kyoto

Not being in Kyoto

Xina   Haneda
8.40pm   ANA 648

*

Fuck these Japanese keyboards.

*

The hollowed-out steaming space you gaze out through,
across to another edge, where on a ledge you'd see,
if I'd lent you my binoculars, a German, or Belgian,
glancing across the lowest reaches of a sky,

huffing with the breath of a coiled subterranean stream,
the volcano's thirst never quenched, always
threatening new conquests – a bushman's fear
of a yellow tide from the north,

or the T'ang's worry about the hordes
to the north and west, restive traders wanting entry
into markets across the shimmering desert
that's still sifting through small towns

on the edge of countries. This is not the fertile
soil of Aso's plains, the paddies
abutting on houses, clumps of them like
crews of stumps, and the green plains

where battle scenes from the north
of a hundred and forty years ago
were glazed onto celluloid, featuring
Tom Cruise – gadgetised culture, which makes

poets like Harold Stewart or Robert Gray
unnerved: try reading their poems of Japan
modernising, mimicking the Straya
they'd put behind them. The concrete

and cars and transistors and modish dress
spoil the idyllic Asian getaway
they'd planned on, or tossed over, with tiny,
compliant ladies, servile ancient Japs

in a quaint island theme park – an inverted
Gold Coast. Postcards, digitised images,
stickers, the air abuzz with frequencies
we don't quite hear or see, humming,

up close, like a dragonfly. And peering
over the caldera's edge –
it stinks. Nearby: the largest *sakura* tree
in all Kyushu

*

Crossing New Canterbury Road,
I'm scanned by the fat shadow
of a JAL airliner.

*

I've found – I think – photos
online matching your description
of Japanese ravens in the park.

Here, as the groundsmen tarp
the cricket pitch before shadows
retreat across the damp, the currawongs

flit between oaks hosted from England,
singing out the wind and the rain
in the dark part of the morning.

The crows' deep, dark cawing
is what struck you, and their massiveness,
the fat wedge of beak like the shadow
behind a door.

*

Facebook chat keeps freezing – were your feet wet
and cold all day in Ueno or Asakusa?

*

*I keep thinking of things
to tell you during the day
and now it comes to it
I can't remember anything!*

*

How many times
did I fish my mobile
from my pocket
to text you?

*

Half of the toilets here are squat.
I find that really backwards
and really disgusting.
Xina says

that apparently it's healthier
to empty your bowels
in an upright position.
I keep pissing on my feet. Sigh.

*

Saturday morning, coffee
with schnapps. On my cup,
an image of *The Great Wave.*

*

Dogen –

Also, Japan is a remote, isolated country;
the people are extremely ignorant.

*

Sheep. The Japanese are like sheep.
They need to be told everything.
I think that's why society

works so smoothly.
But they lack common sense.
Will expand on this another time.

It's really safe here. No one
locks up their bikes.
You can leave your bag in a store

and no one will steal it.
There's no graffiti.
We walked down a trendy street

last night and there was graffiti.
Xina said it was probably fake,
put there on purpose!

No one beeps the car horns.
So it's very quiet.

*

Scanning your photos
for a single glimpse
of Fuji —

I go to the book
Julieanne gave me years ago,
100 Views of Mt Fuji,

and marking the beginning
of the text, I've used
as a bookmark a soft-focus

but perfectly-centred image
of the mountain from Tokyo's suburbs,
clipped from the bullet train,

surrounded by a dim reflection
of my ex-wife's face
as a travelling schoolgirl.

*

Dogen —

The years of a lifetime are a flash of lightning;
who clings to objects?
They are empty through and through.

*

'A Parrot on a Flowering Branch', Hiroshige,

The parrot gripping a near-
vertical branch
is a faded lorikeet —

I wonder what Hiroshige
would've made, say,
of coupled lyre birds

chiming to each other
on the Jamieson Valley forest floor,
unfussed by two pairs

of tourists. This last night
of daylight saving,
I'm leafing, no, flicking

through the book, hardly
looking with intent –
then, 'Crane and Marsh Grasses'.

*

'Crane and Marsh Grasses', Hiroshige,

I think of two pairs of plover
at night on a damp bowling green.

*

You tell me how much
you liked the poem
about my friend's funeral –

we're walking along a cliff-top,
past Echo Point, the edge railed-off,
obscured by a line of trees.

Ten days later, you're
in Japan, scouring the streets
for a single tree:

no mulberries, willows, magnolias,
only cordoned-off miniatures,
small apertures into the shifting world.

*

At night, from a high vantage
an intersection in Tokyo

road almost empty of cars.
Clumps of pedestrians

at each corner waiting for the lights
to change – one blurred impatient strider,

jacket flapping behind,
pacing his own regime.

*

Hi.

I need you to pay my rent for me please.

Hope thats ok?

Weather was shithouse yesterday.
I mean really really bad.
Rain and about 10 degrees.

And we were both really really tired,
beyond humaness. Nevertheless

we went to Kitchenware Town
and saw heaps of fake plastic food.

Wanted to see the fish markets
this morning but were just too tired
to get up at 430am,

as we were beginning
to be worried about our health.

We're pros on the tokyo tube now.
Complicated system but great
once we figured it out.

Off to Tokyo tower today and then
onto Kyoto. Blue skies today
but still very cold.

Thanks and bye! xx

*

The turtle suspended
from a cord
in Hiroshige's print

on the cover of Campbell
McGrath's *Seven Notebooks,*
meant to be freed

as a *karmic offering,*
has Fuji beneath its breast,
but seems to be gazing

at mulberry leaves – perhaps
cherry blossoms? –
just out of frame.

*

After Basho

Kek kek kek kek kek –
startled on the edge of a deep sleep
by panicked plovers.

The commerce student
looks up from his PS2
at the crescent-moon.

Enraged by poetry,
I circumambulate my flat
like Frank Webb in Callan Park.

The raven vanishes
into the under-storey of brush
across the Hawkesbury.

Walking around Petersham
under the full moon —
what? it's dawn already?

In the thunderstorm,
mid-arvo, currawongs gossip
between the lightning.

Horse and cattle bones
in the overgrown paddock —
the grass and cutting wind.

I walked for miles
and when I stopped,
red frangipani blossoms.

Hugging my knees,
squat on the ground, grieving
for my friend the priest.

The haijin pissed, passed out
on the wet cobbled laneway,
covered in *sakura*.

The raven on the wire
all day in Petersham,
pining for Petersham.

*

Harold Stewart –

Those for whom the main
pleasure of poetry lies in its imagery
and who perhaps derived

some enjoyment from the author's
two previous books will find in this one also
numerous little haiku-like touches;

but here they have been combined
by the architectonic principle
of English poetry

to build a longer
structure out of their
minutely observed images.

*

Home from shopping,
the Dogen book on the couch,
covered in plastic,
spills with sunlight.

*

Tokyo, Osaka, Nagoya,
Kyoto —
those heavy Japanese smokers,

dragging and sucking
on chemicals, their *corrected*
rivers channeled through

interchangeable cities,
the suburbs spreading across
them like lichen

in treeless shade.
Tofu restaurants blossom
with kitsch autumnal leaves;

karaoke is discordant from messy
holes-in-the-wall, singing almost
in key is the *prescribed response*,

or a means of *censoring yourself.*
Their *hanka*, fetishised nature,
slaughters African elephants,

lifting the price of ivory above
Fuji's polluted snow, and towering
over the mountain is Godzilla,

that stylised Samurai.
Sakura filter the air like post-war
fallout, or an anachronistic

meditation practice, where Buddhism's
turned crabby, wheeling itself against
the ancient literary elite,

those thirty-seven landowners
writing poems only to each other,
then getting drunk beneath the moon,

listening to the water echoing
against itself in some pisshead's haiku.
Japan is a factory for weirdness —

dolly girls in public toilets, pastiche
bikers, jackets emblazoned with stars
and stripes, that transgressive icon,

and jail-themed restaurants, *gaijin* women
as small-town celebs, vending machines
stocked with ties, and suddenly in Aso,

you're homesick not for Sydney,
or me, but for Darwin — its red earth,
the humid sky peeling off the ocean,

Kakadu echoing like a long-distance call.
And then I see Russell Drysdale's "Sofala"
in a book on Hill End, and, whoops,

at once my reverie falls away — back here
in Petersham, waiting on your reply,
Facebook chat so slow tonight.

*

Each day so cloudy
not a glimpse of Fuji, except
from your guidebook.

*

Didn't do too much yesterday,
easy going day in Aso.
Got drunk last night.

*

tampons in black bag. old people driving stickers.
dubbed American films.

*

Watching *The Last Samurai* with you
on the couch Easter Sunday afternoon,
It's hard, trying to ignore Tom Cruise,
who knows Custer, in a film

translating Japan through a version
of 19th century Americans – the Civil War
and Indian Wars fresh behind them.
Tom Cruise, the all-American boy,

more Japanese – more extinct –
than the modernising Japs.
In *History vs. Hollywood*, a History Channel
mini-doco featured on the movie's bonus disc,

Tom Cruise, star and producer of *The Last Samurai*,
calls Japan "that small island".

*

The girls. Did I tell you
about the girls yet? And their
relationship to the blokes?
I think this is one for when I get back.

*

The floating torii appears only at low tide —
there you are in wet shoes, the red torii behind,
the rain covering the mud, concrete and air.
The torii is an architect's pi.

There you are in wet shoes, behind the red torii,
moss the tourists slip on: *the not-so-floating Torii.*
The torii is an architect's elaboration of pi.
Layers of torii, gating off the sacred

moss that tourists slip on: the now-floating torii:
behind it, across water: the city, sacred bricks,
layers of torii, gating off the sacred
tarmac. Really, the city faces the shrine,

behind it, across water: the city, sacred bricks,
and a blurry torii in the water.
In reality, the city faces the shrine, seeking
entry, crossing silty water, drifting on muck,

and only a blurry torii in the water.

Gaijin rugged-up in hoodies and scarves
seek entry, walk in silt from the water's drifting muck
to the slow hum of water, the clacking of cameras

and chattering *gaijin*, in hoodies and scarves,
watching lichen and barnacles in a slow climb –
the slow hum of water, the clacking of cameras.
In the thin strip of shadow beneath the arch:

lichen and barnacles in a slow climb up its columns,
that narrow roof sheltering nothing
but the thin strip of shadow beneath the arch:
the floating torii only appears at low tide.

*

Thin stone bridge beneath
a palm-sized magnolia – bonsai
in Bunnings Artarmon

*

Gotta run. Bye!

Broken

At Merewether

At Merewether, the horizon boils
with coal ships, and behind it, a transparent
continent ripples like water across the road
in the desert. But the sand here

is not the sand there — this
golden promise of skin cancer and sex,
of bikinis and ice cream, is not
the red dirt twelve hours inland,

tethered to the drift of silence
and emptiness, the slow
implacable nod of geology. Here,
you can wash the present from your feet

under the open air shower
diagonally across from the kiosk,
where lost children gather, eating
smarties and spending years blinking

with their crows' feet at the pouring sun.

Broken

for Rachel Gough

As early   as the first afternoon
in Broken Hill   it seems easier
or perhaps safer   to start seeing
everything through some   narrower focus

like the windscreen or the passenger window
On the way   from Mildura's sludgy Murray
I take three   or four   photos
of what lies behind us   aiming the camera

at the wing mirror: columns   I suppose
of clouds held there   in the green
plastic lozenge   the size of my palm
or   more obviously   through the camera's

view-finder   the aperture   hidden
snapping   at the screen   of an abandoned
and nameless drive-in   or the rusted
red chassis of an XB Falcon   the dashboard

almost intact   or the diagonals
and layered angles   wire fences   rusting
see-saws   kiosk rooves   sheets of tin
on the ground   sheltering small lizards

and tarmac   exposing
dirt patches   An orchard of metal poles
stands for speakers   carrying the audio track
of movies   no longer   flickering

across this screen   with its gapped teeth
its sun a projector   in reverse
casting those squared   and sliced shapes
back across the weedy asphalt   diverting me

drawing focus away   from these forms
I've not yet made out   like the red soil
that contains   without   containing
its own story   its slow peeling-off

                              from itself
its history   from the entire continent
flakes of geological time   beyond narrative
imagism   or thinking

On Christmas night   in the shade
of the lookout   I try   taking a panorama
series   near the car   When I finally
develop the photos   in the shop

at Norton Plaza   forgetting
their order   I'm slipping them
four-to-a-page   into plastic sleeves

in an album   with a Sino-Japanese
floral motif   bought
at Officeworks Petersham

The retro setting
on your digital camera
renders Broken Hill and the desert

around it sepia-drenched,
more directly representational,
amplifying what's already there.

The washed-out glare,
faded red,
blends the South Broken Hill Hotel

seamlessly into the paved street-front
(the desert a mile behind it),
like in Sidney Nolan's painting,

Agricultural Hotel, I think,
where Sheehan's pub drifts off
into the desert,

or the desert into it,
the background sand indistinguishable
from the sandstone pub in the foreground,

the building looking like an awning
propped over a landscape,
a film set façade,

with its windows
peering from out of nowhere,
or perhaps into itself,

like an apparition of architecture.
The storm late last week
's twisted the pub's awning

like a ring-pull. We take our fistful
of photos and head into Coles,
searching for haloumi and cream.

Reduced to taking photos
of the road as it changes colour
from a mid-hue grey

to asphalty black
and back again,
or snapping away,

the shutter
clacking its beak
at road kill.

The wedgetail
fifty k out
on the Barrier Highway,

coasts to the scrubby
grey-green surface,
looking almost

straight through us,
deeming no threat.
Drinking water

by the litre,
and at stinking
road stop toilet blocks

pissing only a thick
syrupy yellow.
Another photo,

click and point
into the road's
swallowing perspective,

or the flat
saltbush pegged-out
to the horizon:

a range of sanded hills
wilts under the colour
of watered-down lead.

Earth almost
the colour of flame,
the shade,

in a painting,
of burning,
and the sky,

its light bleached
by itself,
drifting across,

a patina,
scattered columns
of smoke,

exhausted
by the act
of rising,

as a small
spot resolves
into not a speck

of ash or dust,
but a wedgetail,
assessing land

against a grid
in its head,
perhaps,

expecting
movement.

Five miles out of town
we pull off the road

I open the gate
close the gate

the green car
startles
roos

We stop still a few minutes
nothing

quiet

I reach into the bag
on the back seat
for your ventolin

and take a swig

Christmas day, near sunset,
scaling the stony hill that seems
to climb itself every small rise

we gain. Creaking over loose stones,
keeping to the fading path as the light
slips further west behind the burnt

orange ranges that make a frightening
demarcation, is just like the slow,
juddering drive in through low scrub

and solidified mud trails;
wading at the edge of heavy seas.
The lights of an approaching car

are still distant ten minutes later
on that straight, invisible road.
We head back down to the car

sooner than we'd like, refusing
the entire view, wanting but not wanting
to risk the descent after nightfall, out here,

with only my nokia 1100's penlight
in that heavy-silent, cracked-open darkness,
its crunch of lightless stars.

Nearly slipping
on the path
in the near-dark

middle-of-nowhere,
your weight
cranks rock

against rock —
a match struck
in an empty hall.

I'm closing the gate behind us
as we leave the Sundown Lookout.

I re-fasten the wire hook
to the fence-post,
and you turn off the ignition.

We stand there at the roadside,
facing the dusk cruising
toward us,

and listen.

This thin ribbon
of road,
the low dun hills
folding over with dark.

There's the sound
of the night

calling out to itself,
catching no response,
not even our breathing,

which nearly stills itself,
which is only the ghost

of each diminishing echo
in the replenishing emptiness.

As the end credits roll
on the early Vincent Price film
we bought in town for two dollars
and just watched

on your laptop,
there's an uncertain padding
alongside the tent.
In the thick night,

we make out the form
of a small wallaby,
nibbling at the dark.
When I nudge you

and whisper, *Look*,
it looks up, too,
at the shapes moving
in the tent's dull light,

and calmly lopes down,
I suppose, to the fence-line
searching out a gap.
A little later, outside

to get lip balm from your car,
there's the shock
of the thick mesh
of light overhead.

We can't pinpoint
the Southern Cross:
it's lost in the black's

rippling glow, and I wonder

if sighting even a meteor
would be simpler
than finding a flash
of actual water in the collapsed

and wide flood-channels
carved as if by quiet
into the depthless red dirt

we tick through like a series
of small stones.

In the Royal Exchange, overhearing talk:
about the drunk who arrived in town on the train
with his mates, armed with a hipflask.
He alighted at Sulphide Street Station, dropped his bag
at the cloakroom and strode through town

into the morning's beckoning sand at the outskirts,
and kept going, they suppose. His four mates, stranded
pissed at the Little Topar, rang him, then texted; no reply,
just those four pings on his mobile in the railway room,
Ken's credit running low, and barely two bars of reception.

the desert's intense saffron   as seen
through the tinted windscreen
the pale blue sky verging grey
cleared of impurities

its slow hot wind   propelling dirt
unseeably
                    a vast sand mandala
always re-shaping itself already

the bodhisattva at its centre
invisible   circled by vortices
of reverent indifference
                         the massive
drifting breeze an evolving *om*   over
before it began   a constant syllable
erasing traces you'd left behind
          footprints   tyre-treads off-road

there's plenty of nothing to see
coursing over the thin sealed surfaces
the road the only apparent pattern

there are odd patches
of stiffened water by the sides of the road
where shade's survived

and quick flashes of cloud   dart out
pale   fleeting birds
hover and stitch or a slimy lotus
drooping already   might

or might not   be seen
as you sketch through
the dry   promising air
of your petulant demand for meaning

silverton's surviving civic architecture:
methodist and catholic churches
gaol   courthouse

council chambers   school
masonic lodge   pub
the outline of another pub

and then corners of houses
jagged like torn card
old homes housing shops

one sells cheaply-set opals
you wouldn't buy as a gift
and cast-iron dragons

Crowded with quiet.
The air carrying the slightest
tang, but cloudless.
The dry heat,

the open lid of the sky
and the clear pale
light I'd never seen.
Horizons shaking,

and distance, or perspective,
creasing and discoloured.
A sort of wreckage
happens to the self:

ideas of myself
become *uncollected,*
unconnected, loose-
leaf, and blown.

I zip the tent
open and go inside
to breathe again.

(Annie Dillard, *Teaching a Stone to Talk*, Picador, 1984,15)

Mindioomballa   the broad creekbed
with an emu in it   curling behind
Silverton from its northwest
a sanction of scraggy trees   between
the town's outline   and the graveyard
its thin crust of earth   where you
listen to your footfall   echoing
in a fusty coffin   the cemetery fence
palings weathered   the thread
so saggy   you nearly walk into it
busy with your camera   recording
in binary code   the sand the colour
of dried blood left out   the dates
on headstones   blurred by wind
and dry heat   as if addition and subtraction
provided an answer   some graves
are simply convex impressions   the earth
returning to itself   or bare planks of bone-
bare wood   ghosts of serifs playing
across the surface   or stones delivered
from masons in Adelaide Thackaringa
Broken Hill   the alloy lettering spilt
onto the hot ground   tracing how the past
grieves for itself needlessly   because
no-one remembers   see the dust-stained jar
in the shade   with its scummy residue of stems
the bleached label bearing a trademark   phased out
before Mad Max fixed Silverton   into that
fictional apocalypse   you can drink cold beer to
and look at the photos in the pub   while checking
your photos   of saltbush shrubs at the cemetery
rising from the dirt like revenants   shading the dips
and mounds where bodies were

the rusting land
littered with defunct place-names
distilled from their solid ores –

Purnamoota   Thackaringa   Round
Hill (Taltingan)   Albion
Tarrawingee   Poolamacca,

Umberumberka   Mundi
Mundi   German Charley's
Old Hotel.

The zoom function
on Google Earth   spooks out
to traces of Milparinka   Tallangatta

Waukaringa   Steiglitz
Maytown   Joadja
echoes of Low Gothic   Tocharian

cities of the Takla Makan
Lotharingia   the Khazar Empire
Duchy of Courland

creases in the earth   creekbeds
runnels   traces of old diggings
and trenches   roadside ditches

viewed as satellite images online
the map looks covered
in paper rot or borer traces

in bark   riddles of streams
once foul with use   depots
for typhoid   *a pest more fatal*
than drink

a pest more fatal than drink: Davenport Cleveland, cited in George Farwell, *Ghost Towns of Australia.*

Before you sight the trees
through the thickened horizon
you know you're nearing
the river or some
body of water   when your windscreen
clear but for that fine smear of dust
begins to thicken with the debris
of bug splatter   for hours
the only insects were maggots
larvating in the skins of roadkill
roos   foxes   was that a wombat?
or if we stretch the definition
to include all arthropods   the spider
living in the plastic shell of the wing mirror
even last week   passing a series
of shallow sheets of water
left from the big storm   a few
mosquitos   tapping at the windshield
not even the slightest thrumming
lighter than passing through the corner
of a light sun-shower that dries instantly

the photos gloss over all this:
their shiny surfaces
all white-bordered and neatness
a convenience   a distrust
of the senses' memory   the eye
flowing easily   over the images
not the static motion   of the car
in the desert   that dream of running
trying to run   your legs refusing
to move in a panic of stillness
then waking in the tent   my leg
off the air mattress as morning heats up
caught in the sheet   even awake
my feet still dreaming   of walking
driving   you shift the angle
of the photo to show it   the light
plays and stretches   elastic
across the surface   like a rapid sun —
its reflection   on a distant car's duco
isolating it for a second   even if
you didn't expect the road had curved
all that way

The Blue Gum

The Blue Gum

for my family

Eucalyptus saligna,
                                          the Sydney Blue Gum.
Local distribution is a strip five or ten k
wide from the south bank of the Hunter
that broadens into a wedge north
of Broken Bay,
                                     covering hill slopes,
gullies, the lower reach of scarps.
Bark, blue-grey as a weeks-old
and tenacious bruise, peels down
in long scrolls, meets the ground
with a muffled kiss,
                                  concealed
by early shadows between the hills
where it reaches through the lower
canopy, disguises the contours
of the drained and alluvial earth.
You get lost out here,
                                       off the path,
and you want to stay lost,
at least a while, before you backtrack,
head back to your bike and pretend
to yourself you're just passing through.
In summer their oil is a bright haze
and a smell you want to be out in.

Carboniferous tree ferns,
compressed and stressed
beyond
 age, get trolleyed off
under the surprising sun
to Newcastle, via the South
Maitland, to sudden export
markets no longer under water
or ground —
                    the surface
of the world's folded
and creased, dried, stretched,
flooded, burnt and cracked
since the coal last saw light
alive:
            the slow coal hoppers
queue the traffic behind
the level crossing at Neath,
ten minutes after choofing
through unsighted bush
from the wound-down colliery,
all the way
                    dropping bits of coal
and tickets we'd collect,
which seemed to turn fossil
in the trackside dust,
                              traces
of a past I'd just missed
by a few years, a lifetime —
born into the present
of chitter dumps, of no local
dog races, of dead mine holes
even careful kids
                    tip into.

A couple of remnant blackbutts
in the empty lot
behind the Osti factory,
a clutch of wattle out of flower —

this is where Darren Fisher
was coughed up,
               but before
the guy who raped and killed him

was bought into custody
                  fairly quietly
despite him squatted on the Post Office roof
with a rifle.

The paint on the trademark's
been stripped and redone —
it's changed hands, names,
and now there are young jacarandas

and an orange tree.

Landslide after midnight, The Gap,
Mt Vincent, 1978 — the tour bus'
return from Sydney delayed
after *ABBA The Movie*.
                             Newcastle
is a coronal glow above the hills
that shape in toward them in the rain,
the sudden show of not-road
where the road was; the bus so tightly
hemmed-in there's no U-turn
to head back the long way
via the grey scrub that flanks
the lake's pendant suburbs,
where heavy metals slip in
from Cockle Creek's sulphide works —
where dead fish silver the night's
surface, an SOS. The bus' wipers,
left on all night,
                   flatten the battery.

Shapes of clouds straighten
their shadows the length of the Sugarloaf Range.

You notice this as your father
backs the Datsun out – so carefully –

to pick up payday's fish and chips
from the takeaway six doors up

around the next corner,
his yellow paisley shirt

moulded tight as a watermelon.

The rattle of keys and change
in his overall pockets
as he rolls out and stands up
from under the white Valiant wagon,
smelling of grease and cologne
in the garage's tight half-light,
my grandmother off roasting
a chicken or something
in the oven. She tightens the dials,
traces of clear oil smudge
the kitchen
    where she's been.

Lot numbers proliferate
along Black Hill Road:
in the ammonia waft
of chicken farms and abattoirs,
they count themselves out
on chipboard and asbestos sheets
stapled or nailed to red gums,
a letter box, a chianti bottle
pronged on a fence spike —
these semi-rural bricoleurs,
their intermittent
                 artistry.

You might glimpse, through
the wefted mail of trees,
a car, caravan attendant, or
the frame of a house,
                 an extinct
animal's ribcage, massive,
lurching from the guessed-at
clearing's dust —
             a slow
accumulation of tissue and skin,
reverse fossil, beerish architecture.

Graded-through five years
earlier — just after John Renshaw
was finished — the access roads
are cattle bars, ditched and lumped
and graveled courses.
                 The sun is bright
on them, they're a watery toffee.
Foxes dangle from their tails

in the disguising moonlight,
when you've broken down
and mobile phones
                        aren't invented yet.
The starter jars like a stutterer,
then a mesothaeliac wheeze.
Your grandfather
                        taps at a door,
and a light
                in a back room
comes on.

The hill that shaded my grandparents' house
near the station on late afternoons
                        is beyond
the limit of maps. Roads siphon out
into creased and fingered white margins –
I scroll and hover the mouse
                             to plot out the grid
of my childhood: the clump of lights
between two hills that your mother
gives a name to; the bush track (it spools
down the hill) your father claimed was once
the main route to the lake when your parents
were courting;
                  nameless, unbuilt towns;
narrow, poplared back roads;
                      bypassed sisters;
unworked mines; discontinued down-lines;
clearings with a clutch of foundations;
grown-over dog tracks.
                  Each place here
calls itself a city: Cessnock,
                Maitland,
Lake Macquarie.
          The maps say
that it's so, but don't show
the municipality of ghosts, the outline
of a child's secret civics.

Blue Gum Creek's a slow mirror
with the sky in it.
                    We watch
as we fish the dead currawong
from the water, leaves
and mud in its beak,
                    a brown
sediment embedding
                        the tongue.
We leave it to be dead
on the cracked sandstone slab —
its gold and black eye
an eclipse of the sun.

Both your parents out for the night,
you fight again with your brother —
it's what you do, you're ten —
and try

      to hang yourself
beneath the house
with a pair of octopus straps
from your bike.

      Later,
your mother

      rouses on you.
She doesn't know

      to ask why.

In the back seat,
                on the way home
after a day at Merewether,
legs twitch with exhaustion and sunburn.
Your sister shuffles, her shoulders
tender.
                Instead of John Renshaw Drive,
at mum's prompting we head
through Minmi, past Black Hill
where her cousin lives a patch of bush away
from Minmi Road —
                then turn on
to the road over the hills,
                shadowed
by Blue Gums. It's not dark yet,
but headlights still clip through
gaps between just-burnt trees
before Seahampton — you can see as far
as the Hexham wetlands, from there
at the corner,
                where the gravel street
coils down to Stockrington's
dumped colliery,
                though you don't look,
because your feet are itchy with sand
that's dried
                but won't come off.
Later, when you sleep,
                you dream
of a seaside of yellow, green
and blue bands piled above the other,
and each of them lurch like lemonade
in the Falcon's boot,

             like the fish and chips
gritty with sand in the tomato sauce,
and you're on the hill,
                so high above
the beach, as, so slowly, a huge wave slides
in and washes your family away.

It's a Thursday night,

                  in the Chelmsford's

bottle shop. Which is a drive-through,

though I've walked.

                A flask-shaped bottle

of Jim Beam, it's dole day.

The guy at the counter is Tony Hindmarch's

older brother – he was the one who gave me

concussion with a swinging-arm playing league,

1983. He asks,

               but means to say,

You got a woman waiting, mate,

                    with the wink

of a perv. I say,

         Yair,

              even though

I mean to drink myself dead-drunk

or thereabouts

             because I don't.

Where that house was that burnt down
on Mitchell Avenue
                    the bones of the house
stayed for months.
Kids jumped the fence after dark
and peeled back the brittle floorboards.
Before the block was cleared
after the auction,
                    polished blue floor tiles
grew from the ash-fed grass.

Half a mile behind the slim run of houses
Neath is,
            the chitter dump,
pale pink-grey pile of tipped and glowing
rubbish from the mines near there –
tail end of the Coalfields' few
decades of utility.
                This was the turn
into the 70s, as far away now
as the Rothbury Riot was then.

One August morning,
                the air a still
and frozen canopy, we started out
on the long bus drive to Taronga
with First Abermain Cubs – first leg
down Kearsley Road. Off to the right,
in the just-light,
                the dump, flacked between
the trees, six months after fire,
                        a forest
of blackened posts in truck-churned earth,
and winter's waste-water by the roadside,
slug-coloured, a budget Somme,
soaked with the sky
                as it begins to open out:
foil-coloured light falls across
Hebburn No.2's chain-gate compound,
across the grey road we're on, laid down,
Akela tells us, in the 30s, by susso workers
brought up from Sydney,
                        or the north coast –
all our blokes underground in the struck and filthy mines.

It hangs on the washing,
it's what the towns all around here want back.
It stinks

       for years. It burns itself up,
endless combustion, even when
there's no more coal or refuse to come.

for Reg and George Bull

What we call the country
is a scatter of loose and planted suburbs
where workers need to live — the outer rim
of cities they hate to go to.
                              Their parks
might edge onto the bush, as often
as not.
            Along Lang Street, the gums
were landscaped in long after
the land was cleared to house the men
who'd die in mines
                              or acquire silicosis,
and their first-born,
                              and the second,
who'd leave school to work in the mines
or join the army to pay the doctors.

The old burnout
under the Deep Creek bridge
sheds its orange panels.
Grass in the engine block,

breeze in it off the water.
Two kids, a kiss,
a forearm half
up a shirt.

Walking home from sport on Friday
someone points out the dog
behind the toilets
                    in the park
breathing with maggots.

The Putty Road –
                    endless return
through night from Camden
in cars always five years,
or ten
          out of date.
Headaches from the curved
unstopping, the wind through door-
gaps; the pinch of the new idea:
seatbelts; the fantale quiz
of faceless words in the front seat.
Driving back last year
from Thirlmere, in the pre-rain
daylight, we found my cousins'
home by the Hume. The bridge
across the wide-ditched, thin-
streamed Nattai.
                    Roads fall away
in the rearview,
the thought-lost past
                    looms
and hoons past, eyes you'd never
remember under hunched brows.
Camden, Windsor, Colo Heights,
a life of unlit bush and pressed-down
hills and out almost home
at Wollombi or Bulga.
                    Hours
vanished and lost their shape in there.
Houselights called towns fall away
west in single file and fade.
There's a vast and lost cartography
in my father's car, most likely

in the boot under something
wrapped in hessian. I won't ever
see him again.

                Once, arguing
with her, that boiled, pointless
marriage, he started to drive us
off Mount Pleasant. I hated
for years,
           it was in my gut.
We were skidding off the shoulder.

In the far-off night,

              past

the Loxford level crossing,
a rumble that's almost subsonic —
fireworks' bottom register,
a stifled fart — a town-long train
boring with freight.

              It does nothing

but continue, and bounces sound
off thickened trees, bridges, air.
Low, heavy and low, it stumbles
along the unlined streets between
houses, between shops, impossible
to pick up in the sharp, bright day,
its jagged cowish light

              that's nearly

a smell.

       It's always coal

in the containers, or worthless traces
of coal, spanned by soiled timber
belted with mined and refined steel.
It travels.

       Then the dog kennels

along Horton Road get set off,
and you can hear them forever,
canine ambulance sirens,

              as if

there were someone to save.

For Mary Elwell

One year into high school
the room I spent 6th class in
burns —
        the whole town knows
and thrums by in Kingswoods,
Toyota Crowns, Falcons, utes,
120Ys.
        Dad heard it at the TAB
and bashed home with nary a win
to get us to come and see.
Mum changes out of her nighty
and dressing gown into something
plainer.
        At the school gates
on Lang Street, there's the sniff
of heated tarmac, a new-laid road,
or potholes filled — as the assembly
area heats; the fire brigade's urgent
disco lighting.
        Mary Elwell
tries to dodge the firemen — it's her
classroom that's burning, fuelled
by the petroleum in the shelves
of opera, jazz and classical records
she trained and hassled ears with
for years —
        they dissolve, out
of sight, into the bright percussion
of fire's motifs, its scratchy time
signatures of cracks, hisses,

                              pops —
her hands shine with soot,

                         black as vinyl.
There's no-one to comfort her,
her proper face drips and falls.
Perhaps she hears someone's parent:
what's her snob fucken music
doin for her now?
                    No-one disagrees.
Who notices, a minute later,

                         or hours,
that there are only dull and hushed-
down embers? Everybody leaves —
the lisp of family sedans away
and the dissipant crowd are a slow
face-out, a stylus stuck fast
on the circling, endless groove
that doesn't keep time,
but stalls.

            Trudy's classes return to normal
after a special assembly, after the tidy,
after the tack smell of plastic drops
into the ground, the pliable asphalt.
If she hadn't told me I was stupid
in front of the class, I'd've told her
I was sorry how much she'd lost, or how
that night the night hummed
                         bright
with silent music.

Night at Sandgate graveyard
is a smear across the dark.
Inside the house, cars on Sandgate Road
spill light wandering through the windows,
pale waves on the wall.
                              Some seem to move
of their own accord.
When we opened the door to house-sit
my brother's home,
                         the lights were out,
the interior an underwater black, the switch
hard to find in the pitch.
                              It felt like something
was there, waiting.
                         I said nothing.
On the train home, two days later,
my girlfriend said she looked into the house's dark blank
and imagined a knife.

It was only ever a couple
of dollars at a time (*it's just
a few bob*) but dad spent hour
after hour

        each week at the TAB,
riding out the result — horses,
trots or dogs.

         Someone at Neath
used to run a book on the local
dogs, punted on the circuit
back of Abermain

          through the scrub
off Cessnock Road. Sometimes,
when the wind was wrong
in summer, one of the uncles
said, *the tip was right on top o ya.*
There was another

        off where
David Street heads into the bush
toward the crawchie hole,
the Coalfields' Depression idea
of seafood. Sacked once-
Welsh miners had to have
something to do.

        He'd come back
nightly with empty betting slips
still to be filled in —
share dividends
in not breaking even, teaching us
early

    how to lose.
Mum *tsk*ed and brushed and rolled
her hair

        or paid us to do it for her,
ten cents a minute.

Glebe Road,
            somewhere close
to the slow cambered rise that curls
through a jag of bush
                  toward
Charlestown: the constricted
Pacific Highway.
                  It seemed
like hours from home,
with my mother driving with her
mother to visit her father's sister,
his family estranged, or him
from them. I never knew, was never
told.
      It's in our blood, though,
cutting off sons
                  like a tourniquet.
They went up the high awkward
steps to Myrtle's door — or
was it Joan — and stayed the length
of the book I flipped through
in the car backseat,
                  happily
neglected, distant already.
Kids, we knew nothing
about our grandfather's father.
Still don't,
            other than, like every
other miner or steel miller
from Wales back then, like everyone,
he came by boat,
                  which is where
he learned to drink.

From the lanes behind houses
the windows are square-framed
solid silver or gold, though inside,
that light is something you look
straight through.

              This is well
after dark; no-one's around
but pulses of taillights, car doors
chunked shut in driveways,
and flywire that complains to open
and snips shut like scissors.
The town's endless,

                      but closed-in
by black rims of hills
to the south, smeared with light
from Newcastle's grid.
The transmission tower
on Sugarloaf ticks its cautious
elevation: mute red, it tells you
time still happens, it hints
at a larger structure.

                It spreads
sitcoms and community
announcements up the valley
until the signal degrades to snow
somewhere near Quirindi.
The news is rarely local, less so
the further you drive

                  from the studio.
Eventually, lights go out like a tv,
first a small pin of light,
then gone.

The First Kurri Cubs file into ANZAC Day:
frost is a wink in the grass of Civic Park,
a glimmer the silver-grey of spent armaments.
A local pipe band cranks through a series
of martial Scots anthems— stirring,
unpopular, so foreign. Sparrows shift
and dart, catching the almost-sun,
brief and silent flashes you pay more
attention to than the solemn

      but parroted

declarations of nation's blood

      and loss,

meaning something less than pride;
and the birds, in this colourless light,
smoked morning, are the shade
of autumn leaves shaking, early to fall.

Open-cut dust is a fine and airborne
lifted silt,
                 a sifted plume
that covers the valley it laid long under.
The mine, gone quiet now,
is a false basin extractor pumps
empty rain from;
trucks bend round manufactured hairpins;
black spaces in the night you drive through,
slapped once with dim noise
                              from below,
like the steam trains that chew and cart
coal through the sliced cutting
                         at Abermain
across from the Denman Hotel, and the cake shop
that sells burgers and seafood today.
It's an early lesson
                    in knowing something
not seen must be there,
                         set under
what you can see, an uncertain strata,
a seam to unprick from darkness with only
guesswork, and your father's quiet,
                              and a map
in your head that followed black main roads
and thin back streets but couldn't
understand where those lines went,
how anything could slip out of sight,
                                   how
could you hear trains
                    and not
                         see them?

How did the night swallow direction?
It was as if
                  your grandfather — your dad's
dad — had never lived, that
                          silence,
that blotted-out dark
                          you didn't know
until you saw, for a moment, that photo —
it shakes in your sobbing father's hand —
of a bald man leant against the fence
and shed
              you knew as a jumble of planks,
rust and cobwebbed half-light,
an unstoried past recessed into your childhood.
His Abermain mines sputtered
                              and gave out
between his death and your getting born,
the years that splinter and dim,
a dark shaft with the sound of crows
and stiff breeze through the she-oaks
replanted by J&A Brown,
                          from the boundary fence
in.

    When Dad drives us to West Cessnock
to watch the last passenger train to clump through
to there, past the back way behind Neath,
                                          all
the way from Newcastle,
                          maybe
there was hope there,
                          in the ending
steam that fell around us

106

                      as mist,
or smoke, in the mid-winter
arvo we shivered into.

Static crackles,

               the dial greasy with fingerprints,
curling between stations. The black empty road,
dark hills in shade, pale moon, the smell
of invisible livestock. You think

                        of the white bones
of cows emerging from dark soil

                  thatched
with long grass, or the curve of a skinny river.
The radio picks up a field of conversations
from a town across the horizon.
The paddocks open out

               beneath the sun,
or the cicadas' white noise crackles half in tune
with your bad reception and breaks up like a marriage.
The sun's always embedded in the chrome strip
between window and door,

                 or the moon is.

Was it always night when the car was moving?
Past rail yards at Hornsby on the way back
from Camden,

             across ridges down into darkened
valleys, prinked with houselights, along Hunter Street
after a relative, unsighted by us kids,

                     in the hospital
that tottered over the beaches, in slow ruin
even then of lino doused with antiseptic, the scent
of massed, trayed food,

                the shuffle of zimmer frames,
the hiss and drop of outdated lifts that heave guts
into your mouth,

            not an illness,
but an unease, like clearing air
over a brief rise in the road, your father just above
the limit, your mum in the mirror a curled glare
at him, and you feel only sick —

                hours-old lemonade
and chips.

        You remember this later,

               when you never
want kids of your own, afraid

            of what you'll do,
of what you'll be, how much like them.

                What you want
is to take your child to a level crossing deep in the night,
somewhere far, flat or bushed-in, it doesn't matter,
and watch

         as the slow bass freight passes, the heavy shiver
of weight on the earth you'll both know, and forgetful
of what hasn't

          passed between you.

1.

Dear Dad,
        you might not know
the jacaranda in your mum's backyard,
the one you climbed to pull me down
when I couldn't find a way,
isn't there anymore.

2.

Honey (both of you),
it goes like this:
to mark Trudy's second birthday:
the slim blue gum
                our father planted
on the east side of the house.
It missed the afternoon sunlight
before it dipped below Neath Hill
earlier than it'd be due
                elsewhere.
Within a couple of years
contracts had been exchanged
and we knew
            we'd never see it climb
any higher into the sky, unless
we were passing by in traffic.
Watch it,
drawn from its plastic tub,
the damp snub cylinder of dirt
it was born to, eased into a shallow
bowl of soil, worms, grass roots,
mum or dad might've mouthed
an awkward ceremony,

knowing.

We had to move the swings
back a bit. We would edge to
and fro in squeaky shade,
a while. Looking ahead to the main
road, tailing back to the chitter dump.
Its grey skin like a tight elephant.
Leaves, olive, a word to learn.
I thought it was a promise.

Now,

we have a daughter of our own,
when I swore in a town not far
from here I'd never.

The satellite vision

says the tree is gone, a lap pool in its place.
But I imagine driving past
with the two of you and swinging back
and knocking on a door, saying who
we were and asking would they mind.
I am longing, I think, for a house,
for a wedge of light,

and time

that might sustain.

Acknowledgements

Many of these poems, in particular the "Broken" sequence, were written with the support of the Australia Council.

A number of these poems have been previously published in *Meanjin, Southerly, Cordite, Mascara, Snorkel, Overland, Island,* and anthologised in *Notes to the Translators* (edited by Kit Kelen) and in *A Slow Combusting Hymn* (edited by Kit Kelen and Jean Kent). "Early Autumn Light" was commissioned by the Red Room Company for its Occasional Poem event. Many thanks to the editors.

I would like to thank a number of readers for their support and for their close and generous attention to earlier versions of these poems: Adam Aitken, Elizabeth Allen, Bonny Cassidy, Judith Beveridge, Jane Gibian, Mark Mahemoff, David Musgrave, Niobe Syme, Lindsay Tuggle, Michelle Weisz, Adrian Wiggins, and Fiona Wright.

This book is for my family.